when bones bloom

sara rian

ISBN978-1-7043-5878-9

This book is dedicated to the boy I first thought I loved 18 years ago and to the man I love now.

• • •

it is magic
when ends
b e g i n.
it is purpose
when hearts
h e a l.
it is survival
when bones
b l o o m.

contents

bones

after losing something
that radiated pure love
i decided it was time
to chip away
anyone or anything
that showed me
any less.

some chew love like tobacco.
others softly place it on their tongues
and pray it won't dissolve too quickly.

just because i knelt on broken glass
long enough to get used to the pain
does not mean i was unharmed.
that was not comfort. it was familiarity.
and it punctured the skin.

the devil you know still injures.

what a relief.
to lick my lips and know
the salt i taste is from the sea
and not from tears you caused.
today i soaked in sun.
not heartache.

when bones bloom

i'd rather sleep next to emptiness
than lie next to pain.

before you pick it.
ask.

will you wait for it to ripen.
and will you miss it if it rots.

just because they left
does not mean
it wasn't love.
just because they stay
does not mean
it is.

i can't let this heart shatter
over bad people.
too many beautiful loves
live inside of it.

i'll always enjoy seeing another's fairytale love.
but i look forward to finding my person
and becoming my favorite
love story.

she admired my passion
and she loved my rage.
but there were times
after reading a poem
she would softly ask me
if i'll ever write gently
about falling in love.
oh momma, if only
you could read
these words
now.

i often forget that you're gone.
then i remember the day
you didn't smile
when i held
your hand.

it even hurts to cut my hair
because i'm slowly taking away
something that your hand has touched.
this is how grief can creep
into the smallest spaces.

when it aches
i quietly tell myself
that we will talk tomorrow.
i know tomorrow never comes.
but it gets me through today.
and i have a lifetime
of todays to go.

holding this grief has taught me
to better hold space for others.
i am thankful for this change.
but in that same grateful breath
i sadly wish i held it better for you.
the thing i learned in losing you
is what i wish i did more in loving you.
and regret digs at the heart you made.

when bones bloom

you were like smoke
seeping through the world's fingers
when it tried to hold onto you.
my only way to keep you
was to breathe you in.
and in my lungs
i can't see you
but you stay
close to my
heart.

sara rian

when i retrace our steps
and sit in the same spot we sat
two months before you left
i wonder if you knew.
if that's why you
held my hand tighter
and your gaze longer.
if you knew it would be
the last mother's day
that my heart would smile
next to yours.

you can do anything.
you've told me my whole life.
getting you back just isn't one of them.
and it's the thing i want most.

a client cried
for her father today.
she waited for my words
to take away her pain.
to convince her that
things would get better.
she doesn't know
i'm wearing the sweater
from my mother's funeral
last year.
or that i sobbed for her
until my eyes swelled
last night.
instead i sat with her quietly.
silently connected to her heart.
and honored her love for a person
as it rolled down her cheeks.

dear survivor of suicide loss,

you've witnessed a harsh reality.
a reality that means
pain can get too big
for someone to stay.
they will always love you.
they will sometimes leave.
two sentences never used
to describe real love.
but in your heart
you know it was.
and you've been left
soaking in confusion.
for now the pretty idea
that those who truly love you
will never leave you
has been destroyed.
and you float in fear
waiting for circumstances
to take something else away.

i see you. *i am you.*

sara rian

you could have everything
you have ever wanted
sitting in your hands
and it still won't
quiet the pain.
or the doubt.
sometimes
holding good things
feels like more weight
when you're drowning.
and it's okay if you feel
both grateful. and heavy.

21

when bones bloom

i cannot imagine a future
without you in it.
so here we are
making new memories
every night in my dreams.

night 218

through my tears i said
i can't come here anymore.
the nightmares hurt too much.
you held me tight and said
you have to, baby.
this is where you see me now.

when bones bloom

<u>night 256</u>

your room was cold
and layered in dust.
with sadness i asked
do you sleep here still?
a tree with twisted limbs
had grown through your mattress
and now canopied the bed.
no, i only sleep in pretty places.
but i know this is where you come to find me.
like the tangled branches
i entwined my arm in yours.
i'm sorry i haven't visited in a while, momma.
relief washed over me when you grabbed my hand.

you've always fought your way back to me, little one.
you always will.

night 284

i found my easter basket before i found you.
filled with chocolate and pink bunnies.
i never thought i'd see one again.
you said you had not forgotten.
it had just been here waiting for me.
with tears i hugged around your neck
and realized we were floating.
you let me collapse and curl onto your lap
and tightened your arms around me.

this is what i do when you cry
even though you might not know it.
i need you to breathe, little one.
it will make it easier for you to feel
me rocking you to sleep.

there is nothing i would need more
when i woke up without you again.

night 418

it had been a while
since i'd seen you.
so i couldn't wait
to hold your hand
and tell you about life.
after hearing about
new stories and love
you reached out
and touched my belly
which for a moment
stuck out far and round.
i told you i was sorry
because it wasn't real
and only a dream.
you smiled and said

it's okay, baby bug. this place is for us.
to see things we no longer can or haven't yet seen.
and i like to dream here too.

night 451

you were wrapped in blankets
surrounded by leaves and a stream.
you looked physically sick in a way
my eyes had never seen before.
i held your hand and asked questions.
how can i help. how can i save you.
you rubbed my hair as i started to cry.
and with a small smile you said

i've always loved how much you love me.
and i know you're scared, baby.
but this isn't your pain to take.
all you can do is promise
you'll never stop loving me after.

night 480

my head was in my hands.
i was crying for you.
you appeared at my side
and handed me a card.
one side was black.
the other was white.
you told me that
you made it long ago
so it would be ready
when you left but
you couldn't give it to me
while you were still here.

black side: *you may not cry every day*
              but every day might hurt.
              i'll be with you for all of them.

white side: *and you'll be in my arms again*
              the day it stops hurting.
              take your time. i'll wait for you.

night 522

my siblings and i running
through a crowded airport.
i don't know where we were going.

you stepped out in front of us
wearing your favorite blue sweater
and our favorite smile.

i fell to my hands and knees. one of us screamed.
you opened your arms wide and said one thing.
hi, my babies.

just like that, we scurried to you.
your four loves wrapped around you like a cloak.
and that was it.

i woke up from our embrace and realized
i haven't hugged my brother and sisters
all at once since the day of your funeral.

when the real world keeps us distant
you've always been the one thing to bring us close.
and even a dream will do for now.

some dreams
are so pleasant.
but there are others.
ones where i'm sobbing
and i'm begging you to stay.
then i must wake up each time
with disappointment and heartache.
how long will this grieving mind take
to accept that i cannot bring you back.
how long will this grieving mind break
this
grieving
heart.

but after so long without you
seeing you in dreams
is worth every tear.

please don't be disappointed
that i still struggle so much with this.
you tried to warn me that you would go someday.
and that i needed to find a way to be okay when you did.
i promise i listened to your attempt to soften the blow.
but i was so focused on keeping you here with me
that i never prepared to let you go.

and if nothing else
today i am thankful
that you were mine
to lose.

july,
you bring a heavy heat
and heavier heartache.
these two things
you'll forever
carry.

how can the world be so ugly?
how can people be so ugly?
her last questions to me.
i quickly tried to tell her
it isn't. they aren't.
i wasn't right and
i wasn't wrong.

that night, i lost her to the ugliness.
in following months, i witnessed it.
yes, i also saw love and support.
but i was shown a new dark
in the world and in others.
i stared into the eyes of
what took her from us.
and i chose to stay.

my body and heart crumbled
but i stayed and kept breathing.
the ugly was wiped out and purged.
it was replaced with hope and vitality.
my growth required such gentleness.
so if it wasn't kind, it couldn't stay.

i eventually stood up and i walked.
into a new life. sadly without her.
thankfully without the ugly.
i can't change that it exists.
or that she no longer does.
but i can choose to stay
and survive.

she didn't take her life.
it was life that took.
it took her peace.
it took her safety.
it took her power.

she did something
that she thought
was the only way
to get those back.

i wanted revenge.
i wanted to share the pain.
i kept my jaw and fists tight.
then i'd think of her sweet smile
and picture her loving hands held open.
a woman so kind to a world that hurt her.
i have a lifetime of learning to be softer.
and i choose to start today.

when bones bloom

after i lost you
mouths would whisper
just wait. time will help.
my body and heart would
clench with resistance.
as though they wanted me
to forget us and betray you.
but they were right. time did help.
it gave me space to honor you.
to learn our new relationship.
to appreciate good love and people.
just as you always wanted for me.
having time was never about forgetting.
it was about putting you
everywhere.

it's as though you planted seeds
but knew they wouldn't bloom
without the grief.
you nurtured and loved
through the hardest times
and knew you couldn't stay
to see them blossom.

you loved me more
than i loved myself.
so with every move
i make in this world
i stop and ask myself
would you be sad
or smiling?

if grief lasts as long as love does
then i will carry both into every life
after this.

when bones bloom

i want to keep my days
rich with laughter and love.
that way when we meet again
i can tell you stories
as we float on the clouds.

and if you cracked open this body's bones
our love would leak from the marrow.
i carry us deep within me.

when bones bloom

i imagine your heaven means wrapping yourself around
every lilac tree that has bloomed this spring.
like you've wrapped yourself
around us every day
since you've left.

this year has held so much.
• i fell in love.
• i fought for justice.
• i started running. slowly.
• i've learned to cherish alone time.
• that dream therapy practice? it's real.
• i wrote another book. you're in it again.
• my hair is lighter than you've ever seen it.
• the weight i carry trying to save others is even lighter.

i know this doesn't capture everything.
i hope next year's list is overflowing.
but something that we won't see
on that list or the next one
is that i finally learned
how to truly be okay
without you
here.

of course
i cry for you
when i am low.
but it is also in
my happiest times
when i pause
and i want
to share them
with you.

and then i think
it was probably you
who put them there.

if i had the choice
to go back in time
and give up all of this
to hold your hand again
i would without hesitation.
but if that option doesn't exist
i instead choose to make you proud.

when bones bloom

that sweet smile
was ground to dust.
and those soft, gentle hands
were taken by the heat and flames.
so please think of her. think of her often.
she can only glow in our hearts and memory now.
please let her. every chance you get.

if a person chooses to speak
to you about a loved one lost
or lets you see their tears of grief
i hope you never lose appreciation
for being handed something so sacred.
that is truly one of life's greatest honors.

it was 2 a.m.
when i got home
from my class reunion.
i snuck into my mom's bed
and we giggled about a boy.
the one i adored when i was 11.
2 months later i lost her.
and 7 months later
i found him.
again.
and i smile knowing that
in the smallest moment
my mother knew him.

bloom

it's a confusing place.
being in grief
and in love.

and just like that
we begin again.
but we do not
start over.

my fear often
holds hands with
my gratitude.
some days
one grips tighter
than the other.
but together
they wander.

the torment i once felt
every time i had to sit alone
has turned into delicious peace.
and sometimes i can't get enough.

every organ, cell, and breath
is filled with the intention
of keeping you here
and keeping you safe.
a person who loves you
should do the same.

the healing i've done
inside and alone
has let me see
true beauty
outside.

look at you.
see what i see.
feel what i feel.
how could i not love you?

if i die tomorrow
i hope it's by a bullet
filled with love and lead
and i mumble my last words
with joy dripping from my mouth.

the ones you love are lucky.
the ones who stay know it.

i was buried alive
but never stopped digging.
handful after handful of mud
i clawed myself up and out.
there may be dirt in my lungs
but i found sunlight
fresh air and
those kind blue eyes.

when bones bloom

where they bruised
you kissed.
when they took
you gave.
how they hurt
you healed.

word after word
i purged them from my heart
and made room
for you.

you will know a poet has fallen
when they tattoo blank pages
thinking of your love.

i took my first breath
the moment you kissed me.

when bones bloom

they tell you
don't look back.
leave the past
in the past.
yet that glance
over my shoulder
was a glimpse of you
and i saw a love
i couldn't leave
behind.

my little heart
met his long ago.
but it had many years
and heartbreaks ahead.
so did his.
but the aches and pain
would make love so easy
when those two hearts met again.

when bones bloom

i'm not interested in passing time
or admiring nicely-placed features.
i want to burrow through
skin. bones. and small talk
and crawl into your heart.
let's reach such depths
that we could love each other
in the dark for the next 100 years.

sugar cubes melting in cups of hot lemon ginger tea.
knitted *yarn* blankets sprawled across the floor.
spiced scents swirling from dimly lit candles.
fire stained leaves glowing outside.
i love how skin warms skin
on these autumn days.
drinking in moments
before winter
arrives.

i love the taste
of you and me.
salty sweet.
sugar and sea.

the iron in my blood
pulls towards you.
i know you're
magnetic.

eventually
we will bask.
but for right now
block out the sun.
all i want touching my skin
in this moment
is you.

even at nighttime
when you curl up and sleep
facing the window and moonlight
i stay close behind you and place my hand
on your upper back as you drift into your dreams.
a heart like yours deserves to be felt from every angle.

it's a beautiful thing
when two people
who often love too hard
for another to match
find each other
and speak a language
they both understand.

i like the way your blue meets my green.
we see each other in ocean colors.
a deep sparkling love swirling
in our eyes.

grateful for those who left me
because i found myself.
grateful for those who left him
because we found each other.

i wish my angels could have met you.

this love.
calmly fierce.
grounded and free.
wild in the safest way.
i'm madly and sanely in it.

thank you for being brave enough
to let me hold your heart
even after all it's seen.
with fresh wounds
and healing scars.
i can feel courage
beating in my
palms.

when bones bloom

when you hold these hands
passed down to me by my grandma
and you bring out my mother's laugh
your love touches generations
and i've never felt so whole.

even while apart
you've given me a place
for my mind to wander
that is not dark
and is not cold.
you've given me a place
with sunlight
and tulips.
where i see your hands
skim the grass
and my legs.
a place i can go
and feel a love
once lost.

it's real love
when you know
they deserve
the best.
it's self love
when you know
the best for them
is you.

there may be moments
when fear will fill you
and you will wonder
if i love you and
for how long.
remember the answer
will always be *yes*
and *forever.*

you're as afraid of losing me
as i am of losing you.
and that's how i know
we have nothing to fear.

when you tell me
about all the times
they tried to break you
i listen to your words
and i feel so ready
to show you what
real love truly
looks like.

when bones bloom

with a hand shading his sleepy blue eyes
he asked why the sun was shining in.
i smiled at the blinds i left open.
because it looks good on you.

you are everything
my mother said
to wait for.

these same blankets.
once wrapped around my pain.
once wrapped around my mother.
these same pillows.
once soaked in tears and nightmares.
once held her head as she napped.
now they smell like sandalwood.
now they feel like you.
fabric. thread.
fiber. cloth.
cushioning grief.
and housing love.
so many loves.

i know it's not easy
to love a girl in grief.
seeing bright smiles
quickly turn into tears.
swallowing silence
because no words
will soothe her pain.
holding that space
for a person
you've never met.
promising that you
won't leave her too.
i know it's not easy.
but you do it
and you do it well.

and if all he could do
was hold her on his chest
while her eyes poured tears
and she cried for something
she could never have back
then that is exactly what
he was going to do.
this time and
the next.

i am terrified to endure
another heartbreak.
one i'd have to survive
without my mother's arms
ready to catch me.
so i truly thank you
for loving me right
and not being another
hard lesson to learn.

they will be heartache
or forever.
love.
breathe.
and let it unfold.

wait for the one
who will match
your magic.

with crossed fingers
hidden behind their backs
others promised me forever.
and then there is you, love.
crossing your fingers
hoping forever
comes true.

i thought it'd be impossible after death took.
so thank you for making *forever*
feel like a good thing again.
what i once dreaded
you've made me
hope for.

when bones bloom

if we do come apart
and end up like the others
these flowers and ferns will shrivel.
the ones that sprouted inside my heart
from the soil you watered with your love.
the glow and glitter that surrounds me now
will surely darken and fade into a familiar gray.
my sticky sweet poetry dripping with syrup and hope
will harden into tough brittle that will crack teeth.
but even if this happens, i'll never regret
loving and being loved by you.
even if only for one day.
because now i know
i can taste sunsets
and drink music.
now i know
i'm alive.

after seeing the strongest loves leave
moments after they promised to stay
it'd be foolish to expect your heart
to live without fear.
but when you find that person
who fills the air around you
with nothing but love
just breathe. deeply.
until it fills your lungs
and leaves no room
in your chest
for doubt.

when bones bloom

every fear
i've ever felt
dies in
your eyes.

every hope
i've ever had
beats within
your chest.

one by one
i took flaws out of my pocket
and scattered them across your view.
more days passed and they slowly piled up.
different colors. shapes. and sizes.
jagged little stones and rocks.

one by one
you picked each one up and kissed it.
the rough textures smoothed and glossed.
they sat in your hand glowing neon colors.
the edges. once so sharp now looked safe.
i've never felt a need to hide them again.

no one knows what will happen.
we might be wrong about forever.
i could burn these pages someday.
but i hope we're right about us.
i hope i eventually stitch
these poems together
into my very first
book of love.
and dedicate
it to you.

Ryan,

Thank you for everything and it all took time. Luv ya!

-❤-
Sara

when bones bloom

Printed in Dunstable, United Kingdom